A Diary of
Postpartum Depression

35 POEMS

ERIN WALKER

A Diary of

Postpartum Depression

Table of Contents

1

Welcome to the Dark

"Welcome to the dark. You can leave it, but it will never leave you."

I whispered back, "why is it so quiet in here?" The question resounded and died, leaving me fearing, hating, faltering.

I found the tunnel out and climbed the path. There the light stood, regal as it ever was, and as I wandered the glorious forest there was a prick in my chest. There, in my heart, a little black stain, and the evil whisperer saying ever so quietly, "You can never escape."

2

Lying here trying to reach resolution

Since last night in the dark with you

It's like an argument inside

Between where I was going

And where I used to be

The things I know, blurred with doubt

If there's pain, there is a way out

But I don't have a ladder

I don't have sticks and screws

It's hard to make friends

When you can't see *anyone*

The thunder draws me back to sleep

When I know it's time to wake up

3

It's so hard to say out loud

What was so easy to type

I'm hurting and there's no reason

I'm broken, and I want to be fixed

4

I know I'm supposed to,

but why is it,

I don't love you yet?

-to my baby

5

And suddenly I can count my friends on one hand.

6

I feel ill inside

Knowing I'm not enough

That I'll never be a good wife

The best lover

Or a good mother

7

I listen to your muffled snores

And pretend you're talking to me

While the stars are getting brighter

And the sun comes closer to the horizon

Sleep doesn't visit me

And I lay here next to you

Missing you

8

Play

We can't go out and play.

We have to protect our treasure.

We can't go out and play

And over time it is assumed.

We can't go out and play

Because we don't get invited anymore

We can't go out and play

Because come to realize we're unwelcome.

9

Please, I just want a hug

A chat

A game

A smile

To sit with you

And be happy.

10

Sad face on my hand.

Like a lonely little sister

And a lonely little girl

Who doesn't belong

In a fairytale married life.

Lonely sad face hand

Like the lonely sad face heart

Of this stupid little girl.

11

Stay inside and enjoy the stifling air, like a nice hot burner to your skin

The sweet smell of the house you cleaned once this year

All the energy you put into someone who can't put anything back into you

Wanting to get out into the world where everyone's met you but nobody knows you

Rather than stay in this building with one person who loves you and one who knows only you

Trying to make sense of the feeling that I'm so alone,

when I'm finally loved by someone

12

At the end of the night

When we're tired as hell

I begin to think, perhaps

I'm alone in the world.

And again, that feeling

Of my cold blood draining,

Dripping, falling from my body

Tells me I'm passively,

Wanderingly, loosely

Walking toward the end

Of a familiar dark tunnel.

God help me.

13

The Flower

There once was a Flower

who lived in a jolly field,

Her face always upturned

Toward the bright sun,

Her petals the glitter

Of the morning rain

The breeze would come,

And tangle her up

With the kindred of her soul

And their petals would dance

And frolic among each other

A set, a bouquet, a whole field

Full of kindred, happy souls

Then the people came,

And the weed cutters,

And the loud, angry mowers.

And our poor little Flower

Fretted not but had faith

Until the mower, one day

Came and chopped all around her.

It went away,

But she was left all alone.

The breeze blew cold

On her petals

And all her friends were gone.

And so our little Flower,

That precious sunbeam incarnate,

Withered and crumpled,

Turned brown and fell over,

Became crunchy and hopeless,

And died.

And so is the Flower that is left alone.

14

Please – please

Remember me

By your side

Not sleeping

Remember to love me

Because I feel so alone

With the world locked out

Just you and me inside

Can't you see I'm going nuts?

I'm turning into something else?

Bippity, boppity, boo,

The living thing became a carriage.

And the magic turned her back at 12

And she was crushed by the horses

The glamour faded, and forgotten

She rotted on that lonely road.

Don't ask me why I'm sad.

I've come to a place

Where there is no reason

And there are no clear words.

15

It's been an age

Since I've felt loved

Like a woman

I just wish I knew

That I was still

Beautiful to you

16

Go away.

I just want to die alone in my bed.

17

Everybody sees the silly,

Stupid little girl

But nobody can see

The sorrow she is a mask for.

18

I just want to go to sleep

And wake up when everything is better.

19

No one is listening

And no one is reading

And there's no one who cares

About this echo chamber

So, here, in my diary,

That no one reads

I guess I'll say

What's bothering me.

I want to die.

Except that I love you

And I can't in good conscience,

Let my baby grow up motherless

I want to die.

And so desperately to tell you

That I need help

But my lips go mute, and I can't.

I want to die

Like my friendships have died

Like my life has died

And like my dreams, they too, have died.

I want to die

In your arms

When I'm very old

And very happy

But I won't,

Will I?

No, I won't.

No...I won't.

I want to die.

So badly.

Right now.

Right here.

Come get me

I'm dead already

The rain soaks my skin

The blood, the blood

If I were with anyone else,

I'd already be gone.

Listen to me.

Save me.

20

There are times when there is no possible good, no matter its direction, that can lighten the day.

21

I miss sharing a body with you.

I miss watching, feeling

Everything you do.

Cuddling close to you

And going to sleep.

22

Worth It

When you hear that shattering glass--

Then you'll know.

When the rain stops, sudden like,

And my skin goes cold.

When my baby wants mommy

And there's nothing to offer him.

And when you hold my soaked body,

And wash the blood off your legs,

Then you'll understand.

"It's not worth it,"

I said.

And then you'll understand.

23

It's all my fault

That I can't go to sleep

That I can't wake up

That the meaning is gone

That the music has stopped.

It's all my fault

That I'm always here

That I feel trapped

That the world

Is a crappy place.

It's all my fault

That I'm all alone

And nobody cares

Or tries to help

Or wants me alive.

It's all my fault

That I can't trust anyone

That I'm angry with you

That I can't change her

That I can't fix my life.

And it's all my fault

That I left

Because I wanted

To hurt you, to hit you,

To scream, to beat you.

And it'll be all my fault

When the blood from my dreams

Streaks the sidewalk in waves

When the blade falls

When my soul leaves

Nobody will take the blame.

It's all my fault

For having feelings

For trying to tell you

And you're telling me

You understand

But you don't.

You're like everyone else

I ever told my feelings to

Who told me

I can do whatever I want

And if I'm not happy

It's because of me

Like I can just get up

Unbreak my legs

Untwist my tongue

And be happy.

24

It feels so selfish

To want more love

From someone

Who already loves me so much.

God, I feel so lonely.

25

I feel like I'm bleeding to death, and of all those in the room, none have noticed they're walking around in blood.

-for love, the witless cheat

26

There's a bog in my chest

That I want to stab

And watch drain away

27

Wandering in my head,

Two people who are both me

Fight for control,

And the one that can save me

Is also the lazy ass.

Because while I know

That you love me

And I feel so loved,

The lie overtakes the joy of it,

That you don't even want me.

And in that spirit,

My friends don't remember me,

My family doesn't care for me,

I'm all alone,

And you don't listen.

And the world would be better off

Without me.

28

What a mess I've got myself into

Falling in love

Having a baby

Stuff you can't unsee or undo

I feel like this is the happiest I'll ever be

And I'm dying inside

29

It doesn't matter if you find true love

Have kids, overcome your fears, make up with your enemies

It doesn't matter if you make lots of friends

And they won't care if you keep in touch, after long

So what if you said you're sorry for hurting someone you love

It won't matter that you got famous, or rich and successful

As you bleed to death on the marble floor

By yourself.

30

There once was a woman of stone

Who found a nice place to lay among the hills.

She slept in peace with a great river through her heart

That swept away passion, and with it, malice.

It swept away her fears, and with them, courage.

It swept away memory, and with it, the will to live.

It hollowed her insides,

And among those wonderful, lush green hills,

Is a huge cavern, hewn of stone, never to rise again.

31

When I finally found happiness, disaster struck me.

Not the obvious sort, it was supposed to be wonderful.

But it wasn't, and I didn't realize that being tired was just a symptom.

As I laid alone for days and then weeks,

Briefly I wondered if maybe I'm sick.

And the conclusion was, as I thought about ending my life,

That I was just fine.

And that delusion followed me.

It followed me through the abandonment,

It followed me until finally I realized I couldn't fix myself.

And as I held onto the last strands of my own life,

I reached a hand out for help,

And you told me to wait.

So I'm waiting still.

Waiting for love, waiting for my old self to come back...

Waiting to live again.

32

I'm dying inside

And all you see

Is what a downer I am

33

Such a huge part of me is dead

And the rest would be, too

If I hadn't hung onto the cliff

That is the life I have now

34

Everybody's so judgmental

But nobody really wants to understand.

35

You needed me

And that reminded me

Who I am

And what I do

To be that person